25-YEAR

Christmas

MEMORY
BOOK

NORDIC LIFE

*Christmas is the most
precious time of year.*

*This memory book will help you
keep your most precious memories
with you forever.*

This book belongs to:

_____

_____

_____

_____

The Christmas Of
20_ _

Places

People

This year's most memorable gifts

To / From   Gift

_____   _____

_____   _____

_____   _____

_____   _____

_____   _____

_____   _____

_____   _____

_____   _____

_____   _____

_____   _____

_____   _____

Christmas movies watched this year

_____

_____

_____

_____

_____

_____

_____

_____

This year's Christmas Songs

_____

_____

_____

Christmas food of the year

_____

_____

_____

_____

Most precious memories

_____

_____

_____

_____

_____

_____

_____

_____

_____

_____

_____

_____

_____

_____

_____

The Christmas Of
20_ _

Places

People

This year's most memorable gifts

To / From   Gift

_____   _____

_____   _____

_____   _____

_____   _____

_____   _____

_____   _____

_____   _____

_____   _____

_____   _____

_____   _____

_____   _____

Christmas movies watched this year

_____
_____
_____
_____
_____
_____
_____

This year's Christmas Songs

_____
_____
_____

Christmas food of the year

_____
_____
_____

Most precious memories

The Christmas Of
20_ _

Places

People

This year's most memorable gifts

To / From   Gift

_____   _____

_____   _____

_____   _____

_____   _____

_____   _____

_____   _____

_____   _____

_____   _____

_____   _____

_____   _____

_____   _____

_____   _____

Christmas movies watched this year

_____

_____

_____

_____

_____

_____

_____

_____

This year's Christmas Songs

_____

_____

_____

_____

Christmas food of the year

_____

_____

_____

_____

Most precious memories

_____

_____

_____

_____

_____

_____

_____

_____

_____

_____

_____

_____

_____

_____

_____

_____

The Christmas Of
20_ _

Places

People

This year's most memorable gifts

To / From

Gift

_____   _____

_____   _____

_____   _____

_____   _____

_____   _____

_____   _____

_____   _____

_____   _____

_____   _____

_____   _____

_____   _____

_____   _____

Christmas movies watched this year

_____

_____

_____

_____

_____

_____

_____

This year's Christmas Songs

_____

_____

_____

Christmas food of the year

_____

_____

_____

Most precious memories

The Christmas Of
20_ _

Places

People

This year's most memorable gifts

To / From   Gift

_____   _____

_____   _____

_____   _____

_____   _____

_____   _____

_____   _____

_____   _____

_____   _____

_____   _____

_____   _____

_____   _____

_____   _____

Christmas movies watched this year

_____

_____

_____

_____

_____

_____

_____

_____

This year's Christmas Songs

_____

_____

_____

Christmas food of the year

_____

_____

_____

_____

Most precious memories

The Christmas Of
20_ _

Places

People

This year's most memorable gifts

To / From

Gift

Christmas movies watched this year

_____

_____

_____

_____

_____

_____

_____

This year's Christmas Songs

Christmas food of the year

_____

_____

_____

_____

Most precious memories

The Christmas Of
20_ _

Places

People

This year's most memorable gifts

To / From   Gift

_____   _____

_____   _____

_____   _____

_____   _____

_____   _____

_____   _____

_____   _____

_____   _____

_____   _____

_____   _____

_____   _____

Christmas movies watched this year

_____

_____

_____

_____

_____

_____

_____

_____

This year's Christmas Songs

_____

_____

_____

_____

Christmas food of the year

_____

_____

_____

_____

Most precious memories

The Christmas Of
20_ _

Places

_____
_____
_____
_____
_____
_____
_____
_____

People

_____
_____
_____
_____
_____
_____
_____

This year's most memorable gifts

To / From

Gift

_____   _____

_____   _____

_____   _____

_____   _____

_____   _____

_____   _____

_____   _____

_____   _____

_____   _____

_____   _____

_____   _____

Christmas movies watched this year

_____

_____

_____

_____

_____

_____

_____

_____

This year's Christmas Songs

_____

_____

_____

_____

Christmas food of the year

_____

_____

_____

_____

Most precious memories

The Christmas Of
20_ _

Places

People

This year's most memorable gifts

To / From   Gift

_____   _____

_____   _____

_____   _____

_____   _____

_____   _____

_____   _____

_____   _____

_____   _____

_____   _____

_____   _____

Christmas movies watched this year

_____

_____

_____

_____

_____

_____

_____

This year's Christmas Songs

_____

_____

_____

_____

Christmas food of the year

_____

_____

_____

_____

Most precious memories

The Christmas Of
20_ _

Places

People

This year's most memorable gifts

To / From   Gift

_____   _____

_____   _____

_____   _____

_____   _____

_____   _____

_____   _____

_____   _____

_____   _____

_____   _____

_____   _____

_____   _____

_____   _____

_____   _____

Christmas movies watched this year

_____

_____

_____

_____

_____

_____

_____

This year's Christmas Songs

_____

_____

_____

_____

Christmas food of the year

_____

_____

_____

_____

Most precious memories

The Christmas Of
20_ _

Places

People

This year's most memorable gifts

To / From   Gift

_____   _____
_____   _____
_____   _____
_____   _____
_____   _____
_____   _____
_____   _____
_____   _____
_____   _____
_____   _____
_____   _____

Christmas movies watched this year

_____

_____

_____

_____

_____

_____

_____

_____

This year's Christmas Songs

_____

_____

_____

_____

Christmas food of the year

_____

_____

_____

_____

Most precious memories

The Christmas Of
20_ _

Places

_____
_____
_____
_____
_____
_____
_____
_____

People

_____
_____
_____
_____
_____
_____
_____
_____

This year's most memorable gifts

To / From   Gift

_____   _____
_____   _____
_____   _____
_____   _____
_____   _____
_____   _____
_____   _____
_____   _____
_____   _____
_____   _____
_____   _____

Christmas movies watched this year

_____

_____

_____

_____

_____

_____

_____

_____

This year's Christmas Songs

_____

_____

_____

Christmas food of the year

_____

_____

_____

Most precious memories

The Christmas Of
20_ _

Places

People

This year's most memorable gifts

To / From   Gift

_____   _____

_____   _____

_____   _____

_____   _____

_____   _____

_____   _____

_____   _____

_____   _____

_____   _____

_____   _____

_____   _____

Christmas movies watched this year

_____

_____

_____

_____

_____

_____

_____

This year's Christmas Songs

_____

_____

_____

_____

Christmas food of the year

_____

_____

_____

Most precious memories

The Christmas Of
20_ _

Places

People

This year's most memorable gifts

To / From   Gift

_____   _____

_____   _____

_____   _____

_____   _____

_____   _____

_____   _____

_____   _____

_____   _____

_____   _____

_____   _____

_____   _____

Christmas movies watched this year

_____

_____

_____

_____

_____

_____

_____

This year's Christmas Songs

_____

_____

_____

_____

Christmas food of the year

_____

_____

_____

_____

Most precious memories

The Christmas Of
20_ _

Places

People

This year's most memorable gifts

To / From

Gift

Christmas movies watched this year

_____

_____

_____

_____

_____

_____

_____

_____

This year's Christmas Songs

_____

_____

_____

_____

Christmas food of the year

_____

_____

_____

_____

Most precious memories

The Christmas Of
20_ _

Places

_____
_____
_____
_____
_____
_____
_____

People

_____
_____
_____
_____
_____
_____
_____

This year's most memorable gifts

To / From   Gift

_____   _____
_____   _____
_____   _____
_____   _____
_____   _____
_____   _____
_____   _____
_____   _____
_____   _____
_____   _____
_____   _____
_____   _____

Christmas movies watched this year

_____

_____

_____

_____

_____

_____

_____

_____

This year's Christmas Songs

_____

_____

_____

_____

Christmas food of the year

_____

_____

_____

_____

Most precious memories

The Christmas Of
20_ _

Places

People

This year's most memorable gifts

To / From   Gift

_____   _____
_____   _____
_____   _____
_____   _____
_____   _____
_____   _____
_____   _____
_____   _____
_____   _____
_____   _____
_____   _____
_____   _____
_____   _____
_____   _____

Christmas movies watched this year

_____

_____

_____

_____

_____

_____

_____

_____

This year's Christmas Songs

_____

_____

_____

_____

Christmas food of the year

_____

_____

_____

Most precious memories

The Christmas Of
20_ _

Places

People

This year's most memorable gifts

To / From   Gift

_____   _____

_____   _____

_____   _____

_____   _____

_____   _____

_____   _____

_____   _____

_____   _____

_____   _____

_____   _____

_____   _____

Christmas movies watched
this year

_____

_____

_____

_____

_____

_____

_____

_____

This year's Christmas
Songs

_____

_____

_____

Christmas food of the year

_____

_____

_____

_____

Most precious memories

The Christmas Of
20_ _

Places

People

This year's most memorable gifts

To / From   Gift

_____   _____

_____   _____

_____   _____

_____   _____

_____   _____

_____   _____

_____   _____

_____   _____

_____   _____

_____   _____

_____   _____

_____   _____

Christmas movies watched this year

_____
_____
_____
_____
_____
_____
_____

This year's Christmas Songs

_____
_____
_____

Christmas food of the year

_____
_____
_____
_____

Most precious memories

The Christmas Of
20_ _

Places

People

This year's most memorable gifts

To / From   Gift

_____   _____
_____   _____
_____   _____
_____   _____
_____   _____
_____   _____
_____   _____
_____   _____
_____   _____
_____   _____
_____   _____
_____   _____

Christmas movies watched this year

_____

_____

_____

_____

_____

_____

_____

This year's Christmas Songs

_____

_____

_____

Christmas food of the year

_____

_____

_____

Most precious memories

The Christmas Of
20_ _

Places

People

This year's most memorable gifts

To / From   Gift

_____   _____

_____   _____

_____   _____

_____   _____

_____   _____

_____   _____

_____   _____

_____   _____

_____   _____

_____   _____

_____   _____

Christmas movies watched
this year

_____

_____

_____

_____

_____

_____

_____

This year's Christmas
Songs

_____

_____

_____

Christmas food of the year

_____

_____

_____

Most precious memories

The Christmas Of
20_ _

Places

People

This year's most memorable gifts

To / From   Gift

_____   _____

_____   _____

_____   _____

_____   _____

_____   _____

_____   _____

_____   _____

_____   _____

_____   _____

_____   _____

_____   _____

Christmas movies watched this year

_____

_____

_____

_____

_____

_____

_____

_____

This year's Christmas Songs

_____

_____

_____

Christmas food of the year

_____

_____

_____

Most precious memories

The Christmas Of
20_ _

Places

People

This year's most memorable gifts

To / From   Gift

Christmas movies watched this year

_____

_____

_____

_____

_____

_____

_____

_____

This year's Christmas Songs

_____

_____

_____

_____

Christmas food of the year

_____

_____

_____

_____

Most precious memories

The Christmas Of
20_ _

Places

People

This year's most memorable gifts

To / From   Gift

_____   _____

_____   _____

_____   _____

_____   _____

_____   _____

_____   _____

_____   _____

_____   _____

_____   _____

_____   _____

_____   _____

Christmas movies watched this year

_____
_____
_____
_____
_____
_____
_____
_____

This year's Christmas Songs

_____
_____
_____

Christmas food of the year

_____
_____
_____

Most precious memories

The Christmas Of
20_ _

Places

People

This year's most memorable gifts

To / From   Gift

_____   _____

_____   _____

_____   _____

_____   _____

_____   _____

_____   _____

_____   _____

_____   _____

_____   _____

_____   _____

_____   _____

_____   _____

Christmas movies watched this year

_____

_____

_____

_____

_____

_____

_____

_____

This year's Christmas Songs

_____

_____

_____

_____

Christmas food of the year

_____

_____

_____

_____

Most precious memories

Notes / Photos / Cards / Recipes

Notes / Photos / Cards / Recipes

Notes / Photos / Cards / Recipes

Notes / Photos / Cards / Recipes

Notes / Photos / Cards / Recipes

Notes / Photos / Cards / Recipes

Notes / Photos / Cards / Recipes

Notes / Photos / Cards / Recipes

Notes / Photos / Cards / Recipes

Notes / Photos / Cards / Recipes